Been N Ur Shoes

Been N Ur Shoes

Christian Inspirational Poems and Spoken Words

Crystal London

Library of Congress Control Number: 2018915019
ISBN: Hardcover   978-1-9845-7394-0
               Softcover   978-1-9845-7393-3
               eBook   978-1-9845-7392-6

Print information available on the last page.

Rev. date: 01/03/2019

To order additional copies of this book, contact:
Xlibris
1-888-795-4274
www.Xlibris.com
Orders@Xlibris.com
789475

CONTENTS

But God Will Heal Your Heart

Remember I was only human, but now I am an Angel. But God.
In my darkest hour I didn't speak out because I didn't think anyone
would understand the pain and torture I
was going through. But God.

Don't think about how short my life was, just remember the good
times we had and the love we shared. But God.
Know that now I am at peace
because I am with our Father and he is beautiful. But God.

Know that I am forgiven. But God
Know that I am in my glorified body living in heaven. But God.
Just know that I am in his presence and I am free. But God.
Know that Jesus welcomed me with open arm. But God.

But God did meet me in my darkest hours.
But God did deliver my soul and brought me home.
But God has promised eternal life and I am here.
But God will comfort you with his love and
the Holy Spirit will minister to you.
But God is here on his throne.

But God is so loving and radiant and because of his power
I am no longer in torment.
But God did send Jesus to resurrect me.
So please rejoice and shout for God is alive and so am I.

One More BREATH

God did it!!!!!!!
God gave me one more breath
One more breath to praise Him
One more breath inside of me
To share of his wonderfulness

One more breath to sing Him Praises
One more breath to say I Love You Lord
One more breath to say Hallelujah!!!!!!!
One more breath to dance and shout
One more breath to speak in tongues
Only God can breathe into me one more breath

A real Man of God! Unbelievable.

I heard a man of God speak yesterday.
I heard in his voice how much he loves
the Lord and the word of God.
I felt the Holy Spirit upon his life.
I sat back to listen to what this was all about.
Is this another church that teaches you the word
that you have already heard?

Or is this somebody that will feed your soul.
Most churches I've been to are about personal gain.
But in this Pastors message well it wasn't the same.

He spoke the truth about how fake some churches are.
Like some churches that, I have been running away from.
It has taken some time for God to answer my prayer,
to find a Holy Ghost Filled church that
leads his people in the right way.

It's sad how some churches rob God's people blind.
This man of God is all about saving your soul,
refueling your soul and saving your life.
I am happy I was invited to come today;
it's been a long time since I shouted with joy and praise.

My heart is once again filled with joy
because God does have men of God out there, fakes no more.
When you get a chance and need a real word from God.
The Church is Rhema Word Ministries please check it out
Your welcomed one and all.
May God continue to bring forth real Men of the Gospel.

At a crossroad?

Are you at a cross road in life?

Is it hard to choose which path to go down?

On one hand you know what's right.

On the other hand you may be thinking, if
I do my own thing I'll go down
this road.

Well, which ever path you decided to go,
please remember that God is on
that same road with you.

He will never leave you nor forsake you.
He will help you get through any
obstacles that may be in your way.

God and his Angels will guide you onto the
path that God had designed for
you before you were born, when you are ready.

Just know that at the end of any road, you
can always turn left or right and
God will be right there by your side.

Best Friends

OMG,
When God made best friends he gave me you.
He knew I would need someone closer
than family to see me through.
God looked into my heart and gave me a piece of you,
We're so connected threw and threw.

How awesome God is to think of me
and choosing a best friend like you.
You are so special to me I could never find enough words.
I thank God for blessing me with you.
You are my sister, my buddy, my spiritual twin;
you are love sent to me from heaven above.

I love you my best friend more than you will ever know.
I hope I show you how much where ever we go.
I am also here for you like you are for me.
My life is so much better because you are a part of me.
I love you girl!

<u>But God promised me this not you!</u>

God promised me anything I ask in Jesus name he will give me.
God promised he will supply my needs and he does.
God promised me a roof over my head and he had provided.
God promised me a job to pay my bills and he has with this one and
Many more to come.

God promised me better opportunities in life
And he has with many more to come.
God is still working in my life to bring me into his next promise
And blessing that I may have forgotten.
God promised me years ago that I will receive
A large lump sum of money, it will come.

God promised me years ago a wonderful husband, he will come.
God promised me a new house, it will come.
God promised me a new car, several have come and gone
but better ones are on their way.
God has promised me a life with peace and happiness, it on its way.
God has promised me so many wonderful things.
Just like a baby everything has to take time to be delivered
And mature for its appointed time.

God's word doesn't come back to him void.
God's word obeys his every commanded and so much more.
God's word never breaks its promise.

6

<u>God will see me through</u>

When facing difficult times in life,
look past what is in front of you and focus on God.
Look past the negative and focus on God.
Push through the hardships and focus on God.

When you focus on God, you start communicating with him.
Telling him all that is between you,
that is stopping your communication with him.
Look past whatever you cannot fix or control.
Talk to God about it and let it go.
Remember God is in control.

He will send you help.
He will pull you through.
He will send his Angels to fight for you.
God is in control of my life.
He loves me so much he won't let go.
How do I know? He tells me so.

I'm so worried

I have faith, but I still worry
I know God, but I still worry
I know that worrying is a spirit that rides the back of faith
I try to remember that my faith cannot break.
I had a situation trying to make ends meet.

I did all I could to borrow, ask, seek for the money I need.
At the last minute my friends did not come through.
I worried how I was going to fix my mistake
That made me worry and blue.

So I bowed my head and asked God to give me his mercy,
His favor and ultimate grace to get me through.
Do you know when it was time to pay that bill
And face an unexpected mistake I made.

Do you know God went before me and deposit his grace.
He deposit his grace in the heart of that man,
Who looked the other way
Because the situation was not that bad.

I thanked God and his Angels above for having my back, when it
Seemed like I would fall this helped me get my faith back.
I will continue to trust God. He is God!

It's ok to cry

*My father, my daddy, my papa, just flew away this morning.
He when up to Heaven to play with the Angels. He was the first
man I trusted, he was the first man who held me tight, he was
the first man to kiss me when I went to sleep at night. He was
the first man that I would run to; he was the first man I loved.*

*He once told me I'll never leave you because I'll be your Angel
above. My daddy got his Angel wings this morning and flew
with the Angels, up to Heaven to be with his father God again.*

*I believe Heaven is a place of love, peace and joy and
I am glad that my daddy is now with the Lord.*

<u>Out of the blue</u>

Where did you come from, out of the blue?
You are so sweet and precious we don't know what to do.
You're a help to others and me, you don't seem to mind.
Anytime we call you, you're right on time.

We love to see your face when you come around.
So sweet, calm and so peaceful, God has given you a crown.
A crown of precious jewels such as you are,
We are so blessed to have you in our lives,
You're an Angel sent from Heaven above.

We love you so very much and appreciate all that you do.
May God continue to bless you.
Thank you!

Somebody lied on Jesus!

People told me that Jesus didn't love me,
Because of the color of my skin.
People told me Jesus doesn't love me,
Because of the relationship I'm in.

People told me that because I don't believe in God
I was going to Hell.
People told me if I committed suicide
That I would go to Hell.
Have they been there?

People told me that I would never be forgiven
For any of my sins.
Well someone lied on Jesus.
From his experience a lie crucified him.
Jesus died for me and washed away my sins.
Therefore, any wrong I do today is forgiven.
And who are you people to judge me?

If I was all bad, why would God have made me in his image?
I love like God (unconditionally).
I'm kind to others just like him. I even forgive.
I love the person he made me to be.
I once turned my back on Jesus because
I didn't think he cared, only
Because people lied to me.

I know for myself that Jesus is just like me.
He loves all people; he will tell and show me the truth.
He does not judge me because he's been in my shoes.
Now I choose to believe that God's love is inside of me.
How can I love another, how can I be blessed, how can I wake up
Every morning feeling my best, how can I laugh, how can I give?
Because love is God and God is! All that I am.

<u>Sunday Morning, time to get ready for church</u>

It is Sunday morning. I need to get up and go to church.
Last night I stayed up playing video games.
All day Saturday I was a couch potato.
Saturday night I went out partying, came home half past 3.

This morning I want to sleep in.
I'm too tired to get up and drive to church again.
I'm lying in my bed looking at the ceiling and I know I am making
Excused about going to church today.

I'm just tired and lazy that's the truth anyway.
But while I am making up these excuses;
I wonder if God made any excuses when I called on him today.

THANK YOU

Thank you God ahead for all that you are doing in my life.
Thank you even for the birds that sing
The trees that give shade in the heat
The air that I breathe
The food that I eat
The warmth of the sun

The water that I drink, swim in and bath in
Thank you for the few friends in my life
Thank you for the family I got ☺
Thank you for the hidden treasures you
give to me each and everyday
Thank you because you know my heart in everyway
Thank you because you supply all of my needs

Thank you for my savior Jesus Christ
Who shed his precious blood for me
Thank you God for setting the captive free
Thank you for healing what's broken inside of me.
Thank you for my life
Thank you, God for everything.

Through it all! I will Praise you God!!!!!!!!

I want to remind myself to Praise the Lord.
Through all of my trials and tribulations
I might take my eyes off of Jesus and on the issues I am facing.

But threw it all God has kept his eyes and hands on me
To guide me through it all.
The key work is through. Through it all, the ups and the downs,
God is right here with me, threw it all.

Oh how I love the Lord. Oh How I love the Lord. Thank you Jesus!
Can't nobody do me like the Lord in the mist of it all.
When my life becomes so hard and it
seems that I can't break through.
God can!!!

He will move mountains, stones, rocks, lava and such.
He will break through it all, to get me through.
God you are so awesome! You are so great! You are so mighty!
There is none like you Lord!

Oh How I Love you, my heart leaps with joy!
Just from the thought of knowing and feeling
How much you love me God!
I can't praise you enough for all that you
do for me, seen and unseen.

Through it all I want to thank you.
Thank you God Thank you God Thank you God
For loving me, remembering me, and never leaving me,
Even in my darkest hours.
I love you so much! I Praise your Holy Name, Amen.

Walking on eggshells

My children told me one day
That they feel like I want them to walk on
eggshells around each other.

Well I have learned that you can't walk on eggshells
Because they break into a million pieces.

When you don't express yourself to others because of their feelings
You end up hurting that person anyway.

It's impossible to fix a broken egg.
But it is not impossible for God to make
the broken pieces whole again.
Whole again but brand new. It starts with forgiveness.

Forgiveness for and from everyone involved.
Now you cannot make someone forgive you,
You can only ask them to forgive you.

Life is meant to be lived not hidden or locked up in a room.
We all need our higher power
To help you to understand it's ok to be real.
There are ways to tell the truth without hurting people.
Let's give it a try.
To my children please forgive me for
asking you to walk on eggshells.

I drive a fast car! Zoom Zoom

I GOT MY DRIVERS LICENSE

I BOUGHT A NEW CAR

I DRIVE ON THE FREEWAY OH HOW MUCH FUN.

I DRIVE FAST, I WISH EVERYONE
WOULD GET OUT OF MY WAY

I DRIVE FAST, MY SPEEDOMITER SAYS 180 MPH

I GUESS THAT MEANS I'LL TRY IT AND SEE
HOW POWERFUL IT MAKES ME SPEED

I'M DRIVING UP TO 80 MILES PER HOUR LIGHT TO LIGHT

I WISH THESE PEDESTRIANS WOULD GET OUT OF MY SIGHT

I LOVE TO LOOK BACK TO SEE ALL THE CARS BEHIND ME

I LIKE TO DRIVE FAST

Oh no! oh no! oh no! I just hit a tree

I woke up in a new home

Over 2000 years my Lord and Savior Raised himself from the grave and ascended to our Father in Heaven. How ironic is it that my Savior would honor me to open my eyes in Heaven on this Glorious day, to see his face and praise him and to be in the presence of God and embrace his love and glory.

Thank you to my family and friends. Please remember, To be absent from you is to know that I am in the presence of the most high true and living God.

Rejoice because I made it to heaven... Hallelujah

If you did not hear from the Lord any more what would you do?

What would you do what could you do? Nothing!!
There would be no sun there would be no moon
There would be no light there would be no love.

I would think there would only be stillness. (If that)
You dump and stupid minded people. Wake up there is a God!!
What is your problem?
There is a great and mighty God.

Without God we would not be in existence. Wake up everybody.
You are not in control of your life.
You are not in control of your destiny.
It is all planned and ordained by God.

Because of his mercies
He gives you a will to make choices in the world.
Hoping and praying that you will chose him this day to serve.
But some of us are selfish and blind. (I don't understand).
My God, how can man think and believe
a lie that he created himself.
(I don't understand).
To be continued.

Grateful

1. **GOD is** *Papa and the Manager of creating things.*
2. **Jesus is** *the Son and Healer and lover of Operations.*
3. **Holy Spirit is** *the worker and helper of getting things done.*

1. *God is a good gift giver.*
2. *God is very capable.*
3. *Faith is to picture it done.*

Daily ask:
Father what do you think?
Jesus what do you love?
Holy Spirit what should we do about it?
Sometimes I just sit back and think on the awesomeness of God.

Believe

God said:

It's better for you to believe in me without seeing me.

(Now that is feeding your faith)

I should have said sometime.

We sometimes assume that when we see people
Looking happy on the outside that everything
must be good in their lives.

But,
I should have asked.

I should have just told you about Jesus.
I should have opened my mouth and asked is everything ok.
I should have stopped and listened to you.
I should have told you about Jesus
And what he has done in my life
And reassure you that he will do the same for you and more.

I should have told you that Jesus loves you.
I should have told you that there is nothing he cannot do for you.
I should have told you how much he cares
About what you are going through
And what your thoughts are.

I should have told you that Jesus is the answer
To all of the questions you have.
I should have told you that through
The blood of Jesus that you have been set free.

I should have told you how to fight the enemy.
I should have told you to turn from the enemy
And give all of your cares and worries to Jesus.
I should have opened my mouth and told you.
I should have taught you how to pray.

I should have taught you that you have authority over you enemies.
I should have taught you how to praise God in any situation.
I should have taught you how to worship God.
I should have told you how real Jesus is in my life.
I should have shown you that Jesus is the light.

I should have told you
That God is bigger than any problem you face.
I should have told you before it was too late.

Don't forget about me.

During this time of the year
With all hustle and bustle so near, don't forget about me.
While you're out buying gifts and being so merry,
Don't forget about me.

When you take your children to see Santa
Claus, don't forget about me.
I am the one who was born in a manger
To be the sacrifice for your sins.
I am the one whose blood was shed for you
To be able to communicate with our Father.

I am the one who has forgiven your sins
I am the one who gave you life.
I am the one who promised eternal life.
I am the one who loves you so much.
I am the one who carried you though the red sea.

I am the one who gave you victory.
I am the one who hears your cries.
I am the one who dries your eyes.
I am that I am, God the Father, Jesus the Son and the Holy Spirit
Your comforter, all in one.

Please don't forget about me for I AM CHRIST JESUS!

Good morning,
I want to share a couple of tips for someone who is looking for a job or need to seek God for somethings:

Do a 5 day challenge start with a talk with God and remind him that he promised in his word that he will supply all of your needs according to his riches in glory by Christ Jesus.

Remind him of the promises in the bible, like if I trust in you God you will direct my path.

Then start confessing things to him from your heart.
Like, God thank you for loving me, thank you for forgiving me. Help me in area's you see I need help in and help me to understand. Please allow the Holy Spirit to dwell in me and I in him so I can know you better.
Even though things are not like I want them to be in my life right now Father. You always make a way.

Help me to hear your voice and make my daily life a better one. I trust you Father with my whole heart.
I need to see your mighty hand move in my life today and every day in Jesus name Amen.

Something like that and in every application you fill out ask the angels and guides to direct and plant your application in the proper people's hearts and hands to call you and offer you the positions speedily in Jesus name Amen.

Talk to him in the next 5 days like (I know you can and will do this for me and I thank you Father in Jesus name.
God you are doing what you know is good and right for me in my life today and every day.
Holy Spirit I ask for great favor among the universe and among man in Jesus name amen.)

When you face something you don't understand say My God Is bigger than this and I trust him to make a way out of no way.

Fill out all applications online with agencies. And go to every interview.

Be Bless

OH God

Why do we have to pray for our enemies?
Why do we have to forgive people who hurt us?
Why do we ask you to forgive our sins when we know
Deep down in our hearts that we want that person to suffer?

Why God when I pray and try to ask you to get my revenge
You have me to pray a blessing over my enemy?
Why God?

Why when I pray you won't allow me to curse and hate my enemy
And see them destroyed?
Why God, in my prayers you change my heart to forgive them
For what they have done to me.
Why God?

God answered me and said: Crystal because of your sins
I forgave you.
Because of your sins you thought you hidden from me,
I forgave you.
Crystal for you and I to remain close you must forgive because
I love you.

Crystal you are no different than your enemies.
You maybe someone's enemy and don't realize it.
But I have changed their hearts as well.
Crystal It is written that you shall forgive your enemies
As I have forgiven you.

You shall love your neighbor as I have loved you.
Crystal I want and need you to be in Paradise with me,
But you must forgive and bless not curse
And I shall heal your hurts and your heart.
And so it is.

<u>He Knew!</u>

On the evening of the last supper Jesus

held up bread and broke it and said this is my body.

*<u>**He knew**</u> his body would be broken.*

Jesus took the cup of wine and blessed it and said drink this

for the shedding of my blood.

*<u>**He knew**</u> this would happen before it did.*

Jesus went to pray and asked the Father to take this cup from him.

*Jesus knew already before he asked, that
he would do the Fathers will.*

*<u>**He knew**</u> the sacrifice he was going to
make and he still went through it.*

<u>**He Knew**</u>.

*There is no greater love than the love of
Jesus for his Father, our Father.*

Thank you Jesus

Untying the Knot

Father God, in the mighty name of Jesus, I heard a message from one of our brothers in Christ today, speaking about (Soul Ties).

Father God in the mighty name of Jesus, I break the illegal soul ties from my finances in Jesus name.

Break threw from the soul ties of old financial contracts in the mighty name of Jesus, Amen.

In my life, from my past there were contracts that I signed in HR where jobs were bought out or legal actions taken against them that may have been bought out for whatever reason unknown to me has affected the release of my financial prosperity.

Father I decree and declare that all old debt contracts with my name on it, is broken and void in Jesus name. Soul ties that are blocking my blessings that God has promised me are no longer tied to me and are released and destroyed in Jesus mighty name, Amen.

I decree and declare blessings owed to me that were held up are now free to be released today this hour, this moment in the magnificent name of Jesus, coming from the universe find me and manifest in my life according to God's word and his promise to me, Amen.

I decree and declare that all known and unknown soul ties financially, physically and spiritually that has been blocking my blessings that God has spoken over my life be released and destroyed right now in the name of Jesus.

I decree and declare that all of my blessings that God has ordained for me will find me and come to me easily, frequently and quickly and manifest in my life and in my hands right now in the mighty name of Jesus, Amen. Thank you Father for this knowledge and awakening you presented to me today.

I love you so much. Please continue to forgive me of my sins Father in Jesus mighty name, Amen.

OK....But

*Do you remember as a child you would be
outside playing with your friends?*

*Then all of a sudden your Mother would
yell, come on child it's time to go.*

*Most of the time your reply would be....aww
man. Can we stay a little while longer?*

Mother we were having fun.

Mom would reply: child I said...Let's go now!

*A lot of times we pray for God to move us into a better place
whether it be as a better person, better place or something else.*

*Here at IHP ministry we have been praying
for our own church building.*

*We needed a place to dwell and God
provided, but it was only temporary.*

*God opened another door for us to worship, but
then he said IHP come on it's time to go.*

Our response: But God we are comfortable here.

God said...Let's go now!

*So we pack up and sometimes grudgingly go
because we are obedient to his will.*

What we forget sometimes is that God is taking us to that new place we prayed for and are believing for, (Our new church building).

I don't care how many times God asks us to pack up and go here or there, every step we take is closer to seeing our new church building manifest into our life.

So from now on when God says <u>let's go</u> we will remember as Moses did and continue to walk by faith and not by sight. We will continue to rejoice because God is so worthy and his love for us is unmeasurable.

By faith we might still have to cross over a red sea in order to get to our promise land (our new church building) and so we will. Let's keep moving forward in Jesus name Amen.

More Than I can bear

When we sometimes get bad news one after another and we think
We cannot take it anymore.
Remember the one who bear all of our burdens.
Remember the one who took upon himself the sins of us all.

Remember this was the will of the Father for Him who knew no sin.
You cannot imagine the pain and suffering Jesus had to endure
All at one time.
But he made it though and so will you.

We tend to hold on to bad news,
When Jesus said (all who are weary
And heavy laden come to me and I will give you rest.)

You don't know how much faith you have until you trust Jesus.
You don't know how much he cares until you trust Jesus.
You don't know that the pain our loved ones goes through
Isn't going to be healing and peace for their souls.
You just don't know.

But what Jesus has promised is peace and no more pain
And no suffering when we are with him in paradise.
When we trust Jesus with our all and allow the Father's will
To be done in our lives we will all have peace and eternal life
With the Father.

Lord let your will be done in our lives
And we cast all of our burdens at your feet.
Please take away all the hurt pain and suffering
And replace it with your love, peace, comfort and joy.
In Jesus mighty name Amen

I'm not going to go to my funeral

By the time you come to see my body

I will be already at rest.

By the time you come to lay my body to rest

I am already in Paradise.

By the time you get the call that I have pass

I am already with the Lord.

No more tears unless they are tears of joy.

No more sorrow nor pain because my soul is healed in Jesus name.

It's Sunday Morning!

This morning I decided to go to church.

*I decided to go to worship with the other saints and
hear the word and hear the word of God.
Something I have been looking forward to all week.*

*I'm looking into the mirror making sure that my
hair is in place, my attire is comfortable in case I
start jumping and shouting during worship.*

*I pray before I leave home that the Angels of
the Lord and my Guardian Angels are with me
protecting me from things seen and unseen.*

*I have this strange feeling inside of me that I am
going to hear a word from God today.*

It's Praise and Worship time I'm so excited.

*I hear a strange noise like gun shots I see people falling. I
guess they are falling under the Spirit of the Holy Ghost.*

*Hey I see an army of Angels around the church covering their
wings over people's souls and lifting them up quickly. Hey
my Guarding Angel has carried me into the arms of Jesus.*

*Jesus! You are so beautiful, when I woke up this morning I had no
idea that I would be in your presence and here I am in Heaven to
worship you and the Father. Oh how wonderful and excited I am.*

I felt no pain I had no fear only joy once you appeared.

*Thank you Jesus, I knew you had a word for me today. I could not
have imagine that the word would be seeing you face to face.*

Between a rock and a hard place

Hummmmm,

Well because of my love and deep concern for someone I love.

*I see this person is involving me in a situation where
I am caught between a rock and a hard place.*

*This makes me feel not like myself. This makes
me feel uncomfortable and unhappy.*

*This situation has put bitterness and
uncomfortable feelings in my heart.*

*Well, I was thinking about how I am feeling between this
rock and hard place, which I did not create for myself.*

*It has taken my joy away. It has taken myself
away. I don't like my feelings and thoughts.*

It has moved me away from my faith.

It has disrupted my life and the life of my family.

*Well, I have decided today is the day that I give this
situation to God. Because he is bigger than it and
he sees and knows all that I am not aware of.*

*I will allow God to pull me out of this spot because I cannot
move freely. I cannot rejoice freely. I cannot forgive freely.*

*I choose to let go of the situation and allow God to
have his way in this person's life and mines.*

<u>For this battle is not mine, it's the Lords.</u>

Thank you Jesus for all that you do for me, I am thankful and grateful for you and I ask for your forgiveness because of this situation it seems that I have turned my back on you.

I had to remind myself that you are a great and mighty God. I love you.

ONE MORE BREATH

God did it!!!!!!!

God gave me one more breath

One more breath to praise Him

One more breath inside of me to share of His wonderfulness

One more breath to sing Him Praise

One more breath to say I love you Lord

One more breath to say Hallelujah!!!!!!!

One more breath to dance and shout

One more breath to speak in tongues

Only God can breathe into me one more breath

<u>Feeding your faith</u>

*Feeding your faith is simple for most of us. It is simply
to trust God in all things, in all situations.*

*Feeding your faith is communication with
the Father in prayer and praise.*

Sometimes we have to be force feed to learn how to trust God.

If someone has a need today should I wait until tomorrow to help?

If someone has a need today should I wait until tomorrow to help?

*I walk into Jack in the box today while
waiting for my car to be serviced.
This young black man around 30 walks up in
front of me to ask for a cup of water.
So then I ordered my food.
I get my food but before I sat down I looked over at the guy. He is
sitting at a table with his head down on the table. I walk over and
say, excuse me are you hungry? Would you like something to eat?
He looked at me strangely and then I said I have more than enough
would you like to share what I have or do you want your own?
He answered; can you buy me a breakfast Jack, please. I
reached into my purse and gave him $4 dollars. He said thank
you and then he said some people just don't understand.
I answered, well I have been in your shoes so I know,
God bless you. then I went back to my table to eat.
As I was eating I'm having this conversation with myself, I
was thinking that he's going to need lunch and dinner for
today to give him energy for the rest of the day. The young
man got up to put his trash away. I called him over.
He says to me thank you again, how can I ever repay you? I told
him just pray for me, my name is Crystal. He said his name is
Sylvester third generation. I asked him what need do you have
today. How can I help you? I mean what need do you have
that I can pray for? So God can supply your need. He didn't
answer but you could see on his face that he was thinking.*

*So I told him I was thinking should I put this $20 dollar in
church tomorrow or should I help someone in need today?*

He had a need today so I gave him the $20 dollars he again
said thank you and he also said again how can I ever repay
you? And once again I said just pray for me, my name is
Crystal. Before he left I told him that he inspired me today.
I needed something to write for church tomorrow and I
needed the Holy Spirit to help me with the subject to write
a poem or spoken word. He put Sylvester in my path.
So my message today is when someone has a need they
may have a need that moment that day that hour and all
you can offer is a prayer. A pray can reach God's ears and
God's heart. You never know how you can help change
someone's life by just praying for them at that moment.
God wants you to remember how you were in a place in your life
and you had a need and God fulfilled your need. So if you can
help please do. You don't have to be homeless to have a need
we're always trusting God to meet our needs and he does.
So please follow the leading of the Holy Spirit.
Because the funny thing is another young man came
in and I grabbed my purse because he didn't look
to safe worthy, God always brings people into my
path to bless I'm sure he does that in yours.
God bless you and may he continue to supply your
every need in the mighty name of Jesus.

*Last Sunday the Pastor spoke about pruning the bonsai tree
because it always looks so beautiful. And what happens
to the parts of the tree that had to be cut off? those pieces
fall to the ground and someone will sweep them up and
throw them away. the tree had no more use for it.
Can you imagine God pruning our hearts? Every time it is
broken every time it feels sadness. Can you imagine God holding
your heart in his hand and pulling out everything from the
root that has made your heart feel so heavy and unhappy?
every hurt and pain we go through God is always
there to heal our heart. our heart is a wonderful
connection to our Father. It saddens him to see all
of the broken pieces of our heart in his hands.
when we let go of the memories of what or who caused our
heart to hurt then we can allow God to pour his love into those
hurting places. he can mend our hearts, he can give us joy
he can help us to forget the pain that our hearts once felt.
God knows our heart, he has a heart as well,
his heart has been broken also.
is there any way for us to help heal God's
heart when he has suffered?
Can we prune Gods' heart? we have to love him. we
have to worship him and we have to praise him.
we have to thank him for healing us. we have to
remember he is God and he created us to love
and worship him with all of our heart.
So if our hearts are in pain sometimes it is hard to worship
our Father. But if we remember that he feels what we
feel then we also need to know that he will heal us.
God never fails us, but we do hurt his heart sometimes and
we are sorry and he is always so faithful to forgive us.*

THE CROSS WE SOMETIMES CARRY

When it feels like the world is on your shoulders and you have no place to unload your burdens, please trust God and lay the burdens and weight at the cross or at the feet of Jesus.

If your shoulders are not built to carry the weight of the world. Trust God. Jesus has already carried the cross for us, so we won't have too.

Your body was built for you to stand strong hold your head up high shoulders back. When you let go and Let god. You ask for his help and solve one issue at a time. All problems have an answer.

In all things trust God. In all things ask Jesus for help and ask the Holy Spirit for wisdom, knowledge and understanding.

GOD IS SO AWESOME.

I JUST HEARD ABOUT ANOTHER AWESOME MIRACLE.
I AM SO HAPPY FOR YOU AND YOU'RE FAMILY.

WOW. GOD'S WILL BE DONE IN OUR LIVES.
HE SUPPLIES ALL OF OUR NEEDS.
HE IS THEE ON TIME GOD!

WOW! CAN'T NOBODY DO ME LIKE JESUS!
CAN'T NOBODY DO ME LIKE THE LORD!

WE PRAISE YOU FATHER WE REJOICE IN YOUR FAVOR=

WE LOVE HOW YOU GIVE US FAVOR
ON MAN'S HEART AND MIND.
PRAISE YOUR HOLY NAME!!!!!!!

OVERWHELMED!!! GIVE ME A BREAK! PLEASE!

GOD IS STILL PULLING ME THREW ALL OF THIS MESS.
GOD WILL STILL SUPPLY ALL OF MY NEEDS
ACCORDING TO HIS PROMISE TO ME.
GOD IS BIGGER THAN THIS NEW
PROBLEM I AM FACING TODAY.
WHEN I LOOK TO GOD FOR THE ANSWER, HE WILL
HELP ME GET THROUGH THE ISSUES QUICKER.
I REMEMBER WHEN GOD PULLED ME THREW
LOSING MY JOB, HE GAVE ME ANOTHER ONE
I REMEMBER WHEN GOD PULLED ME THREW
LOSING MY SPOUSE, HE GAVE ME ANOTHER ONE.
I REMEMBER WHEN I DIDN'T HAVE A DIME; GOD
PROVIDED AND OPEN NEW DOORS FOR ME
I REMEMBER WHEN THE DEVIL THREW SO MUCH STUFF
AT ME AT ONCE THAT I FELT LIKE I WAS GOING TO DIE
THEN GOD AGAIN WHO IS BIGGER, BOLDER AND
BETTER TOOK MY HAND AND PULLED ME THROUGH.
MY GOD I WILL CONTINUE TO TRUST
BECAUSE HE WILL PULL ME THREW. GOD MY
FATHER YOU HAVE NEVER FAILED ME.
YOU ARE ALWAYS RIGHT ON TIME
I NOW TURN MY EYES AND MY FAITH TOWARDS
YOU WHO ALWAYS BRINGS ME THROUGH.

OH GOD.

WHY AM I STRESSING OVER SOMETHING
I DON'T UNDERSTAND? Is IT BECAUSE
THIS IS SOMETHING NEW FOR ME?
WHEN I TRY TO PUT THE PIECES TOGETHER
THERE ARE SOME MISSING.
WHAT DO I DO?
WHEN THE PIECES ARE MISSING, YOU HAVE TO GO
FIND THEM TO COMPLETE THE WHOLE PICTURE.
You SHOULD NOT STRESS OVER SOMETHING
YOU DON'T UNDERSTAND. BECAUSE SOMEONE,
SOMEWHERE HAS THE ANSWER.
LOOK, ASK, AND SEEK AND YOU WILL FIND THE
MYSTERY THAT IS STRESSING YOU OUT.
THEN YOU WILL LAUGH BECAUSE YOU'LL
FIND THE ANSWER WAS RIGHT IN FRONT
OF YOU, OR IT WAS AS EASY AS ABC's

I SEE THE FINISH LINE.
I AM ALMOST THERE..
I HAVE TO KEEP ON, EVEN THOUGH I AM SO TIRED.

YES!!!! I finished this race

Wow,
God is good. God is great.
Let me thank God for blessing me with a praying man.
I love to know that my man puts God first
in his prayers and in our lives
I thank God for answering my prayer, when I asked
for a man who treats me as well as Jesus does.
Allow me to jump and shout when I see my man praise the Lord.
Allow me to thank God for teaching my man through
the Holy Spirit, how God wants me to be treated.
I praise God when I look into my man's eyes, see
the tears, and love that he has for our God.
Hallelujah! Praise God! For the man of
God, he has created for me.

I grew up too fast.
I remember when I first meet you; you had such a beautiful
smile. We had a love connection when I looked into your eyes.
Over the years, I tried to stay in contact.
However, time kept flying bye.
I grew up to fast I get married had a family and time really went by.
I thought about you all the time, because you are always in my
heart. Every time I saw your face, I gave you a big o hug.
I looked into your eyes and I would said always
know I love you so much. I knew you loved me just
as much and I was your special little one.
My heart weeps for my loss and my eyes cries for your joy.
No pain, no sorrow, no more.
Rejoice in the lord and be the beautiful Angel that you are.

I love you so much,

This is my life sometimes: a lot of twists and turns, steep slopes and splashes. <u>But Jesus</u> is always there to catch me, lift me up and place me on solid ground.

Think about it

When some of us go to work, we are working
for someone else's dream and vision.

Not ours.

We work to pay bills and enjoy life.
However, if there is a dream or vision within you.
Reach for it and prepare to make that dream come
true. It is never too late to accomplish your God given
talents. What God plants inside of you will grow and
mature. With God, all things are possible.
When God is the head of your dream and your vision,
trust and believe God will see it through.

You've changed? Really?

*Some people think just because they lose weight and no
longer are fat that they have changed. You still have that
face. It seems like your head is connected to a stick.
Sometimes you do not look healthy, you look so sick.
Sometimes you change the look of your body, but
still the inside of you have not changed at all.
Your still ugly, hateful and jealous inside.
I guess it's harder to change; you're insides is where it really
counts. Your outside is only a reflection of what you look like.
The inside is what comes out of your mouth.
It's ok to change your body to make you feel good.
But it is your heart and your mind that needs to change
to. It will make you beautiful inside and out this is very
true. God sees your heart you can't hide from him.
Now leave me alone, I don't need your negative energy.*

OOH LOOK AT HIM!

*I SAW THIS MAN TODAY DAY HE LOOKS SO FINE.
I JUMPED AT THE CHANCE TO ASK HIS NAME; BOY, I
WISH HE WERE MINE. THIS MAN STOOD SO STRONG
AND CONFIDENT; BOY, I WISH HE WAS MINE. I
GATHER UP THE NERVE TO ASK HIM A QUESTION.
I SAID, ARE YOU INVOLVED WITH
SOMEONE. I SURE AM, HE REPLIED.
I ASKED HIM IF SHE WAS GOOD TO HIM. HE
LOOKED AT ME AND JUST SMILED.
HE HAD THIS PLEASANT LOOK ON HIS FACE, I
WONDERED WHY. I ASKED HIM IF HE WAS IN LOVE
HE SAID, WITH ALL MY HEART.
I ASKED IF HE THOUGHT I MIGHT HAVE A
CHANCE. HE SAID, WHO HOLDS YOUR HEART?
I GOT SO BOLD I ASKED HIM OUT, HE FINALLY
SAID YES, ONLY IF I CAN PICK THE PLACE.
I GOT DRESSED UP, I LOOKED REAL FINE, HE
KNOCKED ON MY DOOR, AND HE'S RIGHT ON TIME.
HE SAID I WILL TAKE YOU TO MY FAVORITE
PLACE, A PLACE WHERE MY HEART DWELLS.
HE TOOK ME TO HIS CHURCH!
I WAS IN A STATE OF SHOCKED.
I LOOKED AT HIM AND HE SAID, JESUS WILL WORK IT
OUT. WHAT EVER YOU'RE LOOKING FOR IS NOT IN ME.
IT IS IN JESUS CHRIST, HE IS THE ONLY MAN YOU NEED.
COME ON IN, I'LL INTRODUCE YOU TO HIM, HE WILL
SET YOU FREE. HE WILL SUPPLY YOUR EVERY NEED. HE
WILL ALWAYS BE A COMFORT TO YOU, HE WILL LOVE YOU
UNCONDITIONALLY AND HE WILL NEVER LEAVE YOU.
JESUS IS MY HEART HE SAID; HE IS THE LOVE OF MY LIFE.
HE SAVED MY SOUL AND DIDN'T HAVE TO DIE TWICE.*

*IT'S YOUR CHOICE TOWALK IN AND OPEN YOUR
HEART, HE WILL SET YOU FREE. I FINALLY
FIGURED OUT WHO HE REMINDS ME OF.
JESUS MY SAVIOR I MET LONG AGO.*

**<u>HAVE YOU ACCEPTED JESUS CHRIST AS YOUR LORD
AND SAVIOR? HE WILL NEVER LEAVE YOU ALONE.</u>**

WORK

My Work, my job, my coworkers, the deadlines, the reports:
*All of this I prayed for when I didn't have a job. All
of this pressure I thought I could handle.
All of these people I have to deal with. All of these meetings.
All of the training and the confusion that comes along with a job.
Well I believe that God answered my prayer and gave me
this job because he knew I could handle it. What seems
overwhelming sometimes is a challenge that I will conquer.
When it seems like coworkers are not getting
along, I need to remind them and myself that we
are a team and together we are strong.
We are a TEAM!
Each one of us has excellent work experience to help each
other work towards our common goal. In my interview, I
could not wait to be hired to help this company grow.
Sometimes I think I forget what I came here for.
To be the best team player I could be to help my department
grow. I remembered I promised that I will strive to succeed.
I will do my work with accuracy, pride, and intelligence you see.
Helping others when they are a little behind, I can do this.
Yes I can.
I just need to be reminded, when I get a little
overwhelmed or a little behind.*

When I see my Saviors face.

This morning I took a nap and this afternoon I
woke up and saw my Saviors face! I was so happy;
I was so excited, I am in this beautiful place.
I turned and saw next to me, my Saviors face again.
He was all that I thought he would be and even more, just you wait.
He's more loving, more joyful, more beautiful
than I could have ever imagined. All I could say is
Hallelujah! Thank you Jesus I praise your name.
I fell so much love all around me and a
wonderful peace that I cannot explain.
No tears, no sorrow, no more pain. Then God called my name.
I looked up at this big bright light. I can't
explain it but it was out of sight!
My God embraced me, he held me tight, and then he said
my daughter welcome home come into my light.
Rejoice for me as you lay me to rest, because I'm
really in Heaven rejoicing with the best.

Remember this?

Today is the day that the Lord has made.
There is nothing I can do about other people's problems,
just pray for them and let go. I cannot control what God has
already planned for today, I will just go with the flow.
I can only face what is in front of me today.
With Gods favor, I can do anything.
My strength comes from God when I am weak.
I just have to remember he right here with me.
I will try not to argue, slap and shout.
I will give it all to God who promise he will work it out.
I am getting tired of the same ole things that drain me. If
I remember, I will ask God to renew and refuel me.
I need to start living in Christ because in him
everything around me is out of sight.
I need Gods help to see me through another day,
because he will takes all of my problems away.
The key to my happiness is in the Lord why should I stress when
he handles it all. I love you God for reminding me to put you first.

Wow,
To someone I loved.
I can't believe you took me for granted.
I can't believe you made me cry.
Over a misunderstanding, you took a little bit too far.
I tried to please you in every way.
All I needed was respect, was that too hard to get?
You broke my heart into a million pieces.
God will heal my heart.
I am strong, I will survive, I will move forward with
dignity and pride. I'm sorry our road has to end.
I look forward to just being friends.
I wish you only the best.
I love you, but I deserve better than this.

I won't hurt anymore

It feels like everyone makes fun of me. It
feels like everyone makes me cry.
It feels like nobody like me, no matter how much I try.
I thought people would stop teasing me once I
grew up, but I was wrong. I'm tired of no one
understanding how I feel or how I feel inside.
I'm tired of feeling like something's wrong
with me, well God made me in
His image.
So I cry like him, feel like him, hurt like him, I heal
like him, smile like him, and I love like him.
Well today, I realized that people who hurt me and
call me names aren't happy in anyway.
God who has shown me love and cares for me from Heaven above.
He turns my tears into joy, and the name calling I now ignore.
The joy of the lord has been my strength.
So today, I choose to be stronger, happier, caring and more in love.
I thank God for allowing me to be his image;
because this is how he created me.

Wow, you're awesome!
Your one of God's mighty WARRIORS
He always put you in front of the battle line, because he
knows you will fight to the end and you will win.
Sometimes in a battle, we feel all alone. God
never allows his army to go in a
Battle alone.
Arch Angel Michael on your left Arch Angel Gabriel on your right
There are so many of God's warriors around you in this fight.
Stand tall, stay strong, stay focus and fight. God chose the best
to win this fight. We are more than conquers in Christ Jesus.
Victory is yours at the end of the fight.

Why do you say to people?
When they have trash on the floor, oh excuse the mess.
When their house is a mess, oh excuse the mess.
When the clothes they have on are dirty, oh I have to go change.
When their car is dirty they might say, I haven't had time to wash it.
Why do people make excuses for what is normal to them?

You are my superhero!!!

*It takes so much strength to go through
what you do daily in the hospital.
I don't know if I could be as strong as you.
I hope one day, the doctors find a cure for you. I
am so proud of you for being a trooper.
Keep doing everything the doctors and nurses tell you to
do. I really admire you and I love you so very much.
You are a real SUPER HERO!*

Lord, please keep me in the stable when my flesh wants to run wild.
I will enjoy the beauty of this land that
you have placed my feet upon.

A lot of people and their spirits bring us down and drain us.
We tend to forget that other people's negativity is not our concern.
I will allow others who have issues to vent, but I won't respond.
It is not worth my time and energy.
I will remember that God Is Bigger than all that seems
to be crumbling around me. I will say thank you GOD
for bringing me through this situation that is
Surrounding me today.
I will put my whole trust in God to bring peace in my life again.
My God will move people and obstacles out of my way.
Especially God please remove fear from me. Amen.
I trust you God for making me stronger and supplying
all of my needs according to your promise to me.
Thank you.

Shaky grounds

Sometimes life overwhelms me.
I feel like hiding, running away until life settles.
On shaky grounds to me means: when my body, my insides,
my soul is uneasy about how things are going to turn out.
I guess things I can't control.
For example: paying a bill and having no money,
getting sued and it might not be my fault, getting
evicted, car breaking down and family issues.
People just don't understand me or want to help me out.
I try not to be a burden, but I do need help. I don't
have all the answers. Will someone please help?
I feel like I'm on shaky grounds and I can't stop shaking
or hold onto something that will help me through this.
Most days are good everything is smooth. Then out of
the blue my world starts to shake. I feel like leaving
this place and starting over somewhere else.
But because this world is a small place,
I'm sure I can't erase my fate.
I don't have any answers to what I will do I'll just
explain my situation and ask someone what Ican do.
Someone may have the answers that I need.

FOCUS

*Sometimes our lives go a little smooth and then one day
someone or something will throw a wrench in. Sometimes
it is hard to handle, control, fix or just leave alone.
That is when I need to allow and remember God's words
to me and his promise to me. God will help me and keep
me strong through this issue I am facing today.
I can do all things through Christ who strengthens me.
I will not fail in whatever this wrench is that
I am facing. I am not facing it alone.
For God is with me. He will never leave me
nor forsake me. God is my source.
I will trust in the Lord with my whole heart and lean not
unto my own understanding. I will rejoice in the Lord
because he has made my crooked path straight.
He is God in my life.
I will focus and continue to Believe God and Praise his Holy Name.*

Because GOD IS!!!!!!!!!!!!!!!

"I forgot to say I'm sorry"

My friend died today
We had a disagreement Time went by so fast
I forgot to call and say
I'm sorry.
I forgot to say, I still Love you
I forgot to say, our friendship is worth more
to me than a stupid argument.
Now that my friend is gone
My heart grieves, because I forgot to say, I'm sorry.
To my friend, I'm sorry for the way I behaved
I love you and I miss you
Be blessed in Heaven with God and his Angels

IM' STILL WAITING FOR MY TURN.

Oh my God!

I have been told for years to wait on the Lord. Wait to be blessed.
Wait for my prayers to be answered. To
just be still and wait on the Lord!
My turn is coming, my change is coming,
and my promise is coming.
However, while I have been waiting, I have known that
in my everyday life, the Lord has blessed me with a
place to lay my head, clothes and shoes to wear.
I am in my right mind; I laugh, cry and dance.
I even enjoy the sun, moon, stars, ocean, mountains,
birds, trees, and wind when it's hot in the desert.
I have been provided with transportation to get me
to and from my destination. He has provided me
with food, drink, fellowship and even money.
I also have peace and God's favor on my life.
He has given me love and his Angels to protect me. He has comfort
me when I felt like giving up. Because I'm still waiting on the lord.
I once remember someone saying, God is
always on time. The Lord never fails.
So why am I still waiting?
Awww man, wait a minute.
He has always been here with me, blessing me.
He has been waiting on me to see if I had known him.
You promised you would never leave me nor forsake
me. You also promised that you would supply all of
my needs. f m so sorry God for being so selfish.
I will continuously praise your name and bless you.
The wait I thought I was waiting for had been
over when you came into my life.
I have seen you do many miracles for me.
I have even felt better when you touch me and healed me.

*I am so sorry that I was blind and could not or would
not allow myself to see you right next to me.
I Love You so Much. I just want to Thank
you Lord! My wait is over!
Praise the Lord!!!!!! Hallelujah!*

Crystal London
livangelcreations@gmail.com

FOR IMMEDIATE RELEASE

A Powerful Dream Inspires New Book, 'If I'm Crystal London, Then Who Are You?'

Crystal London's new book carefully considers the mysteries and complexities of life that are sometimes revealed in dreams.

Carson, California, May 13, 2018 – When author Crystal London had a vivid dream that stirred her deepest emotions and conjured up past trauma, she was compelled to write down and expound on what she remembered. Her new book, based on those writings, is called 'If I'm Crystal London, Then Who Are You?'––an homage to the message, lessons and validation that London gleaned when she explored the cryptic details of her unsettling dream.

Rife with imagery and symbolism, London's dream reveals what she believes is a disturbing representation of herself: a disheveled and ghastly "other Crystal," as London refers to her, who exists in a cold steel room crouched in a corner and hiding from life. Shocked at the realization that she was facing a mysterious, dark version of herself, London awoke wondering what actions or inactions in her waking life might have led to the outcome she faced in her dream.

London touches on important issues––bullying, childhood trauma, self-esteem, mental illness, faith and resilience––as she examines the tormented character, part self and part symbol, who inspired her to reflect on her own life and share the hard lessons she has learned about how to keep going in the face of adversity and fear.

"I hope this reads as an inspirational book in some way," says London. "I had this dream, and when I woke up and thought about it, it was so mysterious that I decided to write about it. What do I think people will get out of this book? A wow factor."

Crystal has also written another inspirational short story now available on Amazon Ebooks as well called "If I'm Crystal London, then who are you?"

'If I'm Crystal London, Then Who Are You?' is published in ebook format by eBookIt.com and is now available at popular online retailers including Amazon.com, Barnesandnoble.com and Apple's iBookstore.

Review copies of 'If I'm Crystal London, Then Who Are You?' are available to media contacts upon request. Crystal London is available for interviews.

CONTACT:
Crystal London

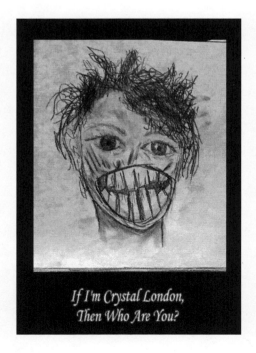

If I'm Crystal London,
Then Who Are You?

Dear Potential Customer,

I am a new, one of a kind "thinking of you" greeting card company called Liv Angel creations.

I have created a keepsake card designed to bring a message from babies in Heaven to their Mother and loved ones on earth.

Mothers that have suffered the loss of their baby or child due to a unfortunate accident for example SIDs, miscarriage, stillborn even in some cases abortions, we often times are still grieving from this terrible loss.

Sometimes the hurt is so unbearable for your friend, wife, mother, cousin, aunt, and sister, sister in law, grandmother or best friend that you don't even realize it.

So I have created a message from Heaven from God's precious Angels to send to their loved ones. My first card simply says "Mommy don't cry, I'm you guardian angel now". I believe that it might be all a mother might need to hear from their baby to start healing her heart.

Thank you,
Crystal London
Creator of Liv Angel Creations keepsake cards.
livangelcreations.com

A Message to you
From Your Baby
In Heaven.

LIV ANGEL
CREATIONS

WWW. LIVANGELCREATIONS.COM

A Message to you
From Your Baby
In Heaven.

LIV ANGEL
CREATIONS

WWW. LIVANGELCREATIONS.COM

livangelcreations@gmail.com

About the Author
This book is dedicated to YOU.

It is intended to inspire you. In all things don't forget God! I have always loved creative writing. I have enjoyed writing books, movies, and plays but never published any until now.

My thoughts come from the Holy Spirit inspiring me with the words to write. Like most people I have been through a lot of struggles and have overcome them by the grace of God.